Practise and Pass
FLYERS

Pupil's Book

**Cheryl Pelteret
and Viv Lambert**

DELTA Publishing

Download the free DELTA Augmented app onto your device	Start picture recognition and scan the **contents page**	Download files and use them now or save them for later

Apple and the Apple logo are trademarks of Apple Inc., registered in the US and other countries. App Store is a service mark of Apple Inc. | Google Play and the Google Play logo are trademarks of Google Inc.

1st edition   1 5 4 3 2 1 | 2026 25 24 23 22

The last figure shown denotes the year of impression.

Delta Publishing, 2022
www.deltapublishing.co.uk
www.klett-sprachen.de/delta
© Ernst Klett Sprachen GmbH, Rotebühlstraße 77, D-70178 Stuttgart, 2022

Authors: Viv Lambert, Cheryl Pelteret
Editor: Kate Baade
Layout: Greta Gröttrup
Design: Typoint, Berlin, Germany
Illustrations: Andy Hammond, Claire Mumford, Grit Döhnel
Cover design: Andreas Drabarek
Cover illustration: Grit Döhnel
Printing and binding: Elanders GmbH, Waiblingen

Printed in Germany
ISBN 978-3-12-501772-6

CONTENTS

Before the exam

Start!

1 ▶ **Match the questions and answers.**

1 ☐ Where can I write the test?

2 ☐ Which papers are in the test?

3 ☐ Do I have to spell every word correctly?

4 ☐ How long does the test take?

5 ☐ What will I get after the test?

a You will get a certificate!

b You can write the test at school, or a test centre near your home.

c In the test, there is Reading and Writing, Listening and Speaking.

d Yes, spelling is very important.

e The whole test takes approximately 75 minutes.

2 ▶ **Circle the correct answer.**

Listening

1 There are 5 / 6 parts.

2 There are 25 / 30 questions.

3 The test takes 25 / 30 minutes to complete.

Reading and Writing

4 There are 6 / 7 parts.

5 There are 34 / 44 questions.

6 The test takes 30 / 40 minutes to complete.

Speaking

7 There are 3 / 4 parts.

8 The test takes 5 / 9 minutes to complete.

Prepare and Practise

To prepare for the test, I can …

- ☐ learn my words
- ☐ practise my spelling
- ☐ do practice tests

and _____ .

On the day

3 ▶ **Say Yes or No. Write the correct sentence for No.**

1 Go to bed early the night before the test.
2 Have a healthy breakfast.
3 Don't be late!
4 Check your bag. Have you got a pencil, rubber, crayons?
5 Take some coffee to drink.
6 Listen to the teacher.
7 Only answer the easy questions.
8 Don't talk to your friends during the test.
9 Ask questions during the Listening test.
10 Try to finish the test before your classmates.

Pass!

Right now, I feel   about the test!

1 Listen and write the words. 🔊 1

1 an ...*umbrella*...........

2 a ....

3 a ....

4 a ....

5 a ....

6 a pair of ....

7 a pair of ....

2 Find the words in exercise 1.

t	i	g	h	t	s	p	s
a	r	b	a	s	c	o	h
r	s	e	m	a	k	c	o
i	g	l	o	v	e	s	r
n	a	t	r	n	g	e	t
g	p	o	c	k	e	t	s
u	m	b	r	e	l	l	a
s	h	r	t	s	e	t	s

3 Read and write the words from exercise 2.

1 It's gold.   ...*ring*...............

2 It's silver.   ....

3 It's red.   ....

4 They're blue.   ....

5 They've got spots. ....

6 They're striped.   ....

It's a stripe / a spot (noun).

It's striped / spotted (adjective).

4 ▸ **Look and write the words.**

businesswoman   fireman   singer
~~footballer~~   journalist   painter

1 *footballer*   2 ....   3 ....

4 ....   5 ....   6 ....

5 ▸ **Look and write the words.**

gold   ~~shorts~~   spot   spotted   umbrella   uniform

1 The footballer is kicking the ball. He's wearing striped *shorts* .
2 The fireman is driving a fire engine. He's wearing
   a ....
3 The singer is singing. She's wearing a .... dress.
4 The businesswoman is walking to work. She's wearing a
   .... ring on her finger.
5 The painter is painting a picture. He's got a big paint
   .... on his shirt!
6 The journalist is holding an .... because it's raining.

6 ▸ **Ask and answer.**

silver belt
a bag with
a black stripe
a uniform
gloves
a big pocket
black tights

striped   shorts

who + is = who's
who + has = who's

7

Step 2 – Practise

1   **Listen and write the names.** 🔊 2

1 ....   2 ....   3 ....   4 ....

2   **Listen and draw lines.** 🔊 3

1 Harry
2 David
3 Emma
4 Emma's mum
5 Robert's dad
6 Peter and Helen

Draw clear lines.

3   **Ask and answer.**

What's Harry doing?

He's playing football.

Step 3 – Pass!

1 Listen and draw lines. There is one example. 🔊 4

Betty Richard Michael Helen

Robert Emma Katy William

Step 1 – Prepare

1 ▶ **Write the school subjects. Listen and check.** 🔊 5

1 *science* .... 2 .... 3 .... 4 ....

5 .... 6 .... 7 .... 8 ....

2 ▶ **Cover the words in exercise 2. Ask and spell.**

How do you spell 'art'?

a-r-t

3 ▶ **Listen and write the words.** 🔊 6

| drums   pyramids   glue   flags   scissors   dictionary   ~~castle~~ |

1 There's a .....*castle*..... on my history book. It's got two ....
2 I'm learning the .... in my music lesson.
3 We learnt about the .... of Egypt in our history lesson.
4 Can I use your .... , please?
5 I need some .... and .... for my art lesson.

4 **Circle the correct words.**

1 It's (midday) / midnight.

2 It's **half past ten / ten to six.**

3 It's **ten minutes past eleven / five to two.**

4 It's quarter **past / to** five.

5 It's **midday / midnight.**

6 It's **quarter past nine / quarter to three.**

5 **Look and write the words.**

This is the Year 6 class. It's Monday. The teacher is **1** _standing_ in front of the board. The subject is **2** .... The **3** .... are sitting at their desks. They're writing an **4** .... Their books aren't on the desks, they're in their **5** .... There's a clock above the **6** .... , and a **7** .... in the corner of the classroom.

Exam
4+2÷3=

Monday,
not monday

6 **Draw lines to match the questions and answers.**

1 What day is it?   It's above the shelf.
2 What subject is it?   It's ten o'clock.
3 What are they writing?   It's Monday.
4 What's the time?   Maths.
5 Where are the students' books? An exam.
6 Where is the clock?   In their rucksacks.

Step 2 – Practise

1 > **Look and write the school subjects.**

9 a.m.	9.45 a.m.	10.30 a.m.	11.15 a.m.	12 p.m.	1.20 p.m.	2.10 p.m.
shiroyt	thams	grhapyeog	cnicese	LUNCH	rat	sumic
history.	....	....	....		....	....

a b c d e f

1 What time does the history class start? *nine o'clock*

2 What time does the art class finish? ....

3 What's the third subject of the day? ....

4 What subject is after lunch? ....

5 What is the last subject of the day? ....

6 What starts at midday? ....

7 What subject starts at quarter past eleven? ....

2 > **Ask and answer.**

What time does the maths class start?

Quarter to ten.

3 > **Listen and circle the words.** 🔊 7

Club: art / music

1 When: Friday / Monday

2 Where: in the art class room / in the sports centre

3 Time: after school / at lunch time

4 How long is the lesson? one hour / half an hour

5 How many students: 14 / 40

1 ▸ **Listen and write. There is one example.** 🔊 8

School

Favourite day at school: ....*Friday*...............

1 How many subjects? ....

2 What time is lunch? It's at ....

3 How long are the lessons? They're ....

4 What are the after school clubs? ....

and ....

5 Favourite thing: ....

Step 1 – Prepare

a

b

c

d

1 ▶ **Match the pictures and the seasons.**

....*c*.... summer   .... autumn   .... spring   .... winter

2 ▶ **Listen and match the pictures from exercise 1 to the names.** 🔊 9

....*c*.... Sarah   .... Michael   .... Emma   .... Harry

3 ▶ **Find these words in the pictures in exercise 1. Look and write.**

1 **folg**   *golf*
                   ....
2 **nett**   ....
3 **thole**   ....
4 **tusiseca**   ....
5 **ksis**   ....
6 **delegs**   ....
7 **namwons**   ....
8 **lalbwons**   ....

> Use going to for future plans!

4 ► **Write the words. Do the crossword.**

		¹t			²	
		o				
³		r				
		c	⁴			
		h				

Across

1 I play volleyball in the school

....

3 What are you going to do tomorrow? Look in your ....

Down

1 You use this to see in the dark. Take it with you when you go camping!

2 Jill's bought a new ....

5 My football team is going to .... the match!

5 ► **Look at the pictures again. Circle the correct word.**

1 They're sleeping in a **hotel / (tent.)**
2 The **magazine / diary** is open.
3 They're playing **volleyball / golf.**
4 Volleyball Team **A / B** is winning.
5 The **score / torch** is 5–2.

Step 2 – Practise

1 Listen and number the pictures in the correct order. 🔊 10

Listen to the whole dialogue, then answer!

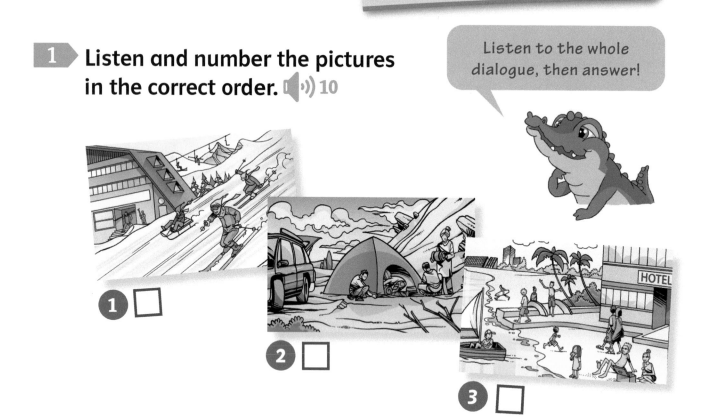

1 ☐

2 ☐

3 ☐

2 Listen. Write A or B in the box. 🔊 11

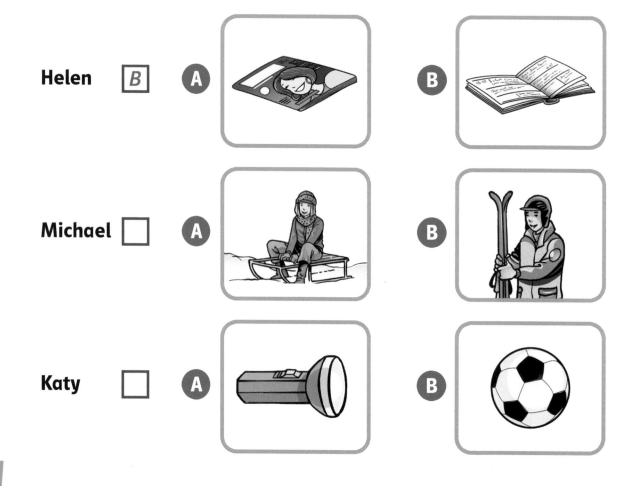

Helen | B | A | B

Michael | ☐ | A | B

Katy | ☐ | A | B

1 People are talking about their favourite holidays
There is one example. 🔊)) 12

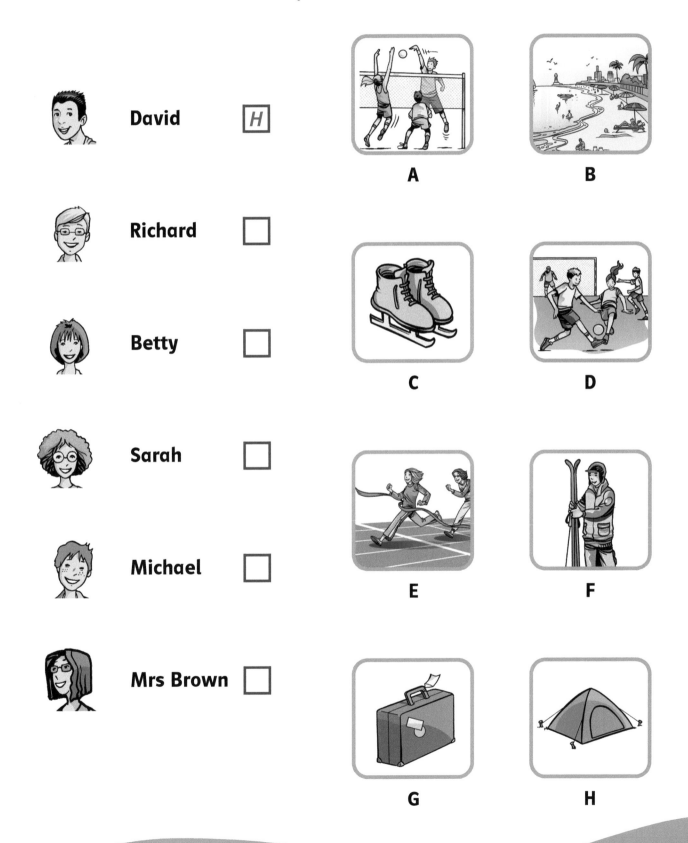

David   H

Richard   ☐

Betty   ☐

Sarah   ☐

Michael   ☐

Mrs Brown   ☐

A

B

C

D

E

F

G

H

Step 1 – Prepare

1 ▶ Draw lines to match the words and the pictures.

1 window

glass

2 stamp

paper

3 scarf

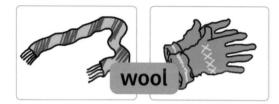

wool

4 ring

gold or silver

5 table

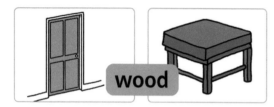

wood

6 comb

plastic

7 key

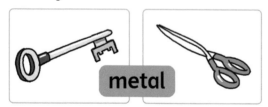

metal

8 box

card

2 ▶ Write the words. Listen and check. 🔊 13

1 Combs are made of   *plastic* .
2 Stamps are made of   ....
3 A key is made of   ....
4 A table is made of   ....
5 Boxes are made of   ....
6 A scarf is made of   ....
7 A ring is made of   ....
8 Windows are made of   ....

3 Find and circle seven objects in the wordsearch.

4 Write the objects in exercise 3 and the materials.

	Object	Material
1	*brush*	*plastic / wood*
2	....	....
3	....	....
4	....	....
5	....	....
6	....	....
7	....	....

5 Think of the materials. Circle the odd one out.
Listen and check. 🔊 14

1	stamp	magazine	(hat)
2	newspaper	window	glass
3	comb	uniform	toy
4	cooker	desk	fridge
5	box	birthday card	CD
6	T-shirt	scarf	sweater

1 ▶ Listen and tick ✓ the box. 🔊 15

> Listen to the whole dialogue, then answer!

A ☐    B ☐    C ☐

2 ▶ Listen again and tick ✓ the box. 🔊 16

1 John was **on a swing** ☐ **in the garden** ✓ when he found the bag.

2 The bag was made of **paper** ☐ **plastic** ☐ .

3 The box was made of **wood** ☐ **wool** ☐ .

4 The key in the box was made of **gold** ☐ **metal** ☐ .

5 There was a **letter** ☐ **card** ☐ in the envelope.

6 The **stamp** ☐ **comb** ☐ was very old.

1 ▶ **Listen and tick ✓ the box. There is one example.** 🔊 17

What did Jane lose at the swimming pool?

A ☐   B ☐   C ✓

1 Which bowl did William buy for his mother?

A ☐   B ☐   C ☐

2 Where is the telephone in Emma's house?

A ☐   B ☐   C ☐

3 Where did Harry go last summer?

A ☐   B ☐   C ☐

Step 1 – Prepare

1 Circle the correct word.

3 warm / cold

1 left / right **2 friendly / unfriendly**

5 heavy / light

4 low / high

2 Write the opposites of the underlined words and do the crossword.

1 This blanket is so nice and <u>soft</u> – let's sit on it, because the ground is too ....hard.... .

2 Your room is very ....! I like my room to be <u>tidy</u>.

3 This bag is very ....! It isn't <u>light</u>.

4 Is your dog <u>friendly</u> or ....?

5 Don't turn <u>left</u>. Turn ....

6 That <u>high</u> tree is dangerous. Please climb a .... tree.

7 It isn't <u>cold</u> today. It's ....

1 h a r d
2
3
4
5
6
7

3 Ask and answer. Listen and check. 18

What's the opposite of tidy?
Untidy.
How do you spell it?
u-n-t-i-d-y

4 Look and write the words.

bored	different	enough
excited	far	~~horrible~~	lovely
near	same	too little

1 Queen Jane is *horrible* but Queen Anne is ....

2 These books are the .... but these are ....

3 There's .... water in this glass but there's .... water in this glass.

4 Harry is .... but Peter is ....

5 Building A is .... but building B is ....

5 Ask and answer.

What's the opposite of horrible?

Lovely!

6 Write the words.

1 I like your coat. It's ....

2 You've got fair hair, and your brother's got brown hair. You don't look the ....

3 We can't swim to the island. It's too ....

4 I'm .... Let's do something interesting.

5 We can't make a cake. We haven't got .... flour. There's too little.

6 It's Sarah's birthday tomorrow. She's very ....

Step 2 – Practise

1 ▶ **Circle the correct words.**

1 The children are having a (lovely) / **horrible** time in the park.
2 The dog can't get the ball in the lake – it's too **near / far**.
3 The kite is flying **high / low**.
4 The kite is **light / heavy**.
5 The children are having a picnic on a **soft / hard** blanket.
6 The man in the café looks **untidy / unfriendly,** because the boy is playing a drum.

> Listen carefully. Don't colour everything!

2 ▶ **Listen and colour the picture in exercise 1.** 🔊 19

3 ▶ **Look at the picture in exercise 1. Listen and write.** 🔊 20

1 ▶ Listen and colour. Write and draw.
There is one example. 🔊 21

1 ▶ **Write the words and find Jim's job.**

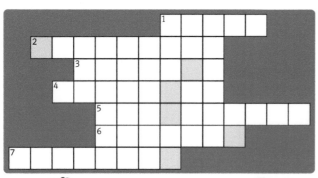
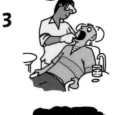

He is an ....

2 ▶ **Look and write.**

1 You go here when you are hungry. ....*café*........... .
2 You travel in this if you don't have a car. ....
3 You visit this place if you want to learn about history. ....
4 You go here if you want to buy medicine. ....
5 You visit this person if you feel ill. ....
6 You can read stories by journalists in these. ....

3 ▶ **Read and write the best jobs for these children.**

1 I want to make people laugh. I want to work in a circus. ...*clown*...
2 I'm going to visit space in a rocket. ....
3 I want to work in the theatre or on television. ....
4 I love flying. I'm going to learn to fly a plane. ....
5 I'm good at cooking. I'm going to work in a restaurant. ....
6 I'll work in an office and write stories for a newspaper. ....

4 ▶ Complete the questions with _How_, _What_ or _Where_.

1 ....*What*........ do you do?
2 .... do you work?
3 .... do you get to work?
4 .... long does it take?
5 .... far is it?
6 .... is the hospital like?

5 ▶ Match these answers to the questions in exercise 4.

1 20 kilometres ....*5*.......
2 I'm a doctor. ....
3 It's very big and it's new. ....
4 40 minutes. ....
5 In a hospital. ....
6 I go by bicycle. ....

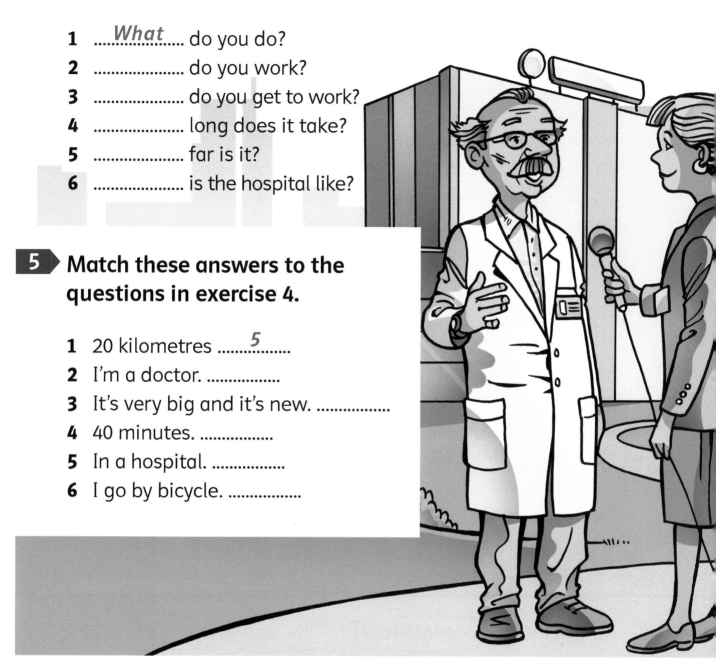

6 ▶ Work with a partner. Partner A, choose a job. Partner B, ask questions.

What do you do?

I'm a waiter.

Where do you work?

I work in a ...

1 Write *T* (true) or *F* (false).

1 A restaurant is a place where you can eat and sleep. ..*F*..
2 You can buy medicine at a post office. ....
3 You go to the station if you want to catch a train. ....
4 A university is a place where you can study. ....
5 A meeting is a meal with meat in it. ....
6 Astronauts are people who work in the circus. ....

2 Look at the letters. Write the words.

1 An **catro** ......*actor*...... works in a theatre.
2 A **nigsre** .... is good at singing.
3 A **rife terifgh** .... works in a fire station.
4 A **regotpor hahp** .... takes photos.
5 A **nedstit** .... helps you if you have toothache.
6 A **tobolafler** .... is very good at football.

3 Circle and write.

1 **an artist / (a police officer)** This person wears a uniform.
   ...*a police officer*...

2 **a footballer / a journalist** This person writes for a newspaper.
   ....

3 **an office / a chemist** Business men and women work here. ....

4 **an airport / a factory** They make cars here. ....

5 **a waiter / a pilot** This person works in a restaurant.
   ....

6 **an engineer / an artist** This person designs bridges.
   ....

Copy the words carefully!

1 ▸ **Look and read. Choose the correct words and write them on the lines. There is one example.**

a pilot

traffic

hotel

an ambulance

a café

a journalist

a newspaper

nurses

an actor

a fire station

a cook

a police station

a bicycle

a taxi

Example

This person flies a plane. ....

Questions

1 You go to the hospital in this if you
are hurt. ....

2 This person writes in a newspaper about
things that have happened. ....

3 Fire fighters work in
this place. ....

4 This person works in a theatre or
on television. ....

5 Police officers work
in this place. ....

6 This person works in a kitchen and
makes meals. ....

7 These people work in hospitals
with doctors. ....

8 This is another word for 'bike'. ....

9 You can have a drink and a snack
here with your friends. ....

10 This is the name for cars, buses, lorries
and motorbikes on the street. ....

1 ▶ **Write the words and find out what Katy is making.**

I'm making ....

2 ▶ **Look at the pictures in exercise 1. Write *H* next to the healthy foods.**

3 ▶ **Talk to a friend. What food should / shouldn't you eat every day?**

You should eat vegetables every day.

You shouldn't eat pizza every day.

4 ► Circle and write the words. Which is the odd word?

1 ....*plate*....
2 ....
3 ....
4 ....
5 ....
6 ....
7 ....

pplatespoonnsaltspepperysnowmanforkcknifets

5 ► Write the words from exercise 4.

1 **Jane:** Have you ever eaten with chopsticks?
   Paul: Yes, I have, but I prefer using a ....*knife*.... and ....

2 **Peter:** This pasta doesn't taste very good.
   Daisy: Would you like some .... and .... on it?
   Peter: Yes, please.

3 **John:** Is the table ready for dinner?
   Mum: I need one more .... for the bread and a .... for the soup.

6 ► Look and write. Then ask a friend.

1 Have you ever ....*eaten*.... (**eat**) octopus?
2 Have you ever .... (**try**) carrot cake?
3 Have you ever .... (**use**) chopsticks?
4 Has your mum ever .... (**make**) jam?
5 Have you ever .... (**taste**) vegetable soup?

Have you ever eaten octopus?

No, I haven't.

1 > **Read and draw lines.**

1 What's your meal like?   We could go to the café.
2 Have you ever eaten here before?   I was waiting for you.
3 What are you going to eat?   It's lovely.
4 What were you doing?   Go straight on. It's on the left.
5 Where shall we eat?   I'm going to eat pizza.
6 How do you get to the café?   Yes, we have.

2 > **Circle the correct words.**

> Read the whole dialogue before you write the words.

Ben: What's your favourite food?
Vicky: I **like / liking** pizza.
Ben: Have you ever **been / went** to a pizza restaurant?
Vicky: Yes, I **have / do.**
Ben: Where **did / have** you go?
Vicky: **I've been / I went** to a pizza restaurant in town.
Ben: What **did you eat / were you eating**?
Vicky: **I ate / I was eating** cheese and tomato pizza and salad.
Ben: That sounds good!

3 > **Look and write.**

> took   ~~make~~   smells   mixed
> flour   long   like

Katy: Did you ......*make*...... that cake?
Jill: Yes, I did.
Katy: How did you make it?
Jill: I .... the butter and sugar in a bowl.
              Then I added the eggs and ....
Katy: How .... did it take?
Jill: It .... one hour.
Katy: It .... good. What does it taste .... ?
Jill: Mmm! It tastes good!

1 ▶ **William is talking to his mum. What does his mum say? Read the conversation and choose the best answer. Write a letter (A–G) for each answer. You do not need to use all the letters.**

Example

 William: What are we going to do at the weekend?

 Mum: *D*....................

1 **William:** What's the restaurant like?

Mum: ....

2 **William:** Where is it?

Mum: ....

3 **William:** Have we eaten there before?

Mum: ....

4 **William:** What did we eat?

Mum: ....

A Yes, we have.

B Yes, I'd like that.

C It's at the corner of the street near the cinema.

D We're going to eat in a restaurant.

E It's very good.

F We ate meat and vegetables.

G How do you get to the restaurant?

1 ▶ **Write the words and then number the months in order.**

☐ J _ _ _   ☐ D _ _ _ _ _ _ _   ☐ J _ _ _

1 J *a n u a r y*   ☐ M _ _   ☐ A _ _ _ _

☐ A _ _ _ _ _   ☐ M _ _ _ _   ☐ S _ _ _ _ _ _ _

☐ F _ _ _ _ _ _ _   ☐ O _ _ _ _ _ _   ☐ N _ _ _ _ _ _

> Write 20th June, but say
> the twentieth of June.

2 ▶ **Look and write the words.**

1 There are 30 days in April, June, September and ....*November*......... .

2 Christmas Day is on the .... December.

3 The day after the 31st January is the .... February.

4 The last day of the year is the .... December.

5 .... , July and August are in summer in Europe.

6 .... is the shortest month.

3 ▶ **Ask and answer.**

What date is it today?

It's the fifth of April.

It's on the twentieth of June.

When's your birthday?

4 ▶ **Look and write *in, on* or *at*.**

1 His birthday is ....*in*.......... July.
2 My birthday is .... 15th October.
3 My party is on Saturday .... six o'clock.
4 I like going to the beach .... the summer.
5 We're going to go on holiday .... August.
6 We got home .... midday.

5 ▶ **Look and draw lines to match the sentence halves.**

1 We can go to the cinema   if it's sunny.
2 We might go to the beach   so I went by bus.
3 I didn't want to walk   so I'll have a party.
4 I started playing football   when I was six.
5 I was walking home   if it rains.
6 My birthday is in March   when I saw Mary.

6 ▶ **Ask and answer.**

What do you do if it rains?

If it rains I watch TV.

What do you do if it's sunny?

I go to the park if it's sunny.

1 ▶ **Circle the correct words.**

1 I forgot my books **so** / if I was late.
2 I brush my teeth **until / before** I go to bed.
3 I was walking home **when / after** I saw her.
4 We can play tennis **so / if** it doesn't rain.
5 He was still tired **after / when** eight hours in bed.
6 I was late **if / so** I ran to school.

2 ▶ **Look and write. Then number the sentences in order.**

> midnight
> found
> walking
> ~~April~~
> coats
> until

☐ We walked in the storm for an hour before we .... a cave

☐ We waited in the cave .... it was dark.

☐ We stopped and put on our ....

☐ 1 One afternoon in .... *April* .... we decided to go for

☐ a walk. We got home at ....

☐ We were .... in the hills when it started to rain.

> Think about which type of word could go in each gap!

3 ▶ **Write the words in order to find the title.**

the storm A hills in ....

1 **Read the story. Choose a word from the box. Write the correct word next to numbers 1–5. There is one example.**

When my friend Helen went on holiday she couldn't take her dog Buster, ...*so*.......... he stayed at our house.

One day, I took Buster for a walk. When we left the house it was dry and sunny, but later it was windy and the **1** .... was black. We were walking up the hill into the woods when it started to rain. 'There's going to be a **2** .... ,' I thought.

Buster wasn't very happy. He didn't like storms. We were walking **3** .... the woods when suddenly Buster ran away. I ran after him but I couldn't catch him. I looked for Buster for an hour and I called his name, but I couldn't find him.

I **4** .... to go home. On my way home I was walking past Helen's house when I saw Buster. He was waiting in front of the door. He was cold and wet and he was still afraid. 'There's **5** .... there, Buster,' I said. 'Come home with me.'

I took Buster home and gave him a delicious meal. He lay down in front of the fire and he slept for three hours.

> **Example: no-one** ~~so~~ **sky decided air month storm through waiting foggy**

2 **Now choose the best name for this story. Tick ✓ one box.**

A walk in the woods ☐

A bad day for Buster ☐

Buster's holiday ☐

1 ▶ **Look and write *will* or *won't*.**
In the future ...

1 There ...*won't*... be any cars.
2 Offices .... be made of glass.
3 People .... go to work by bus.
4 There .... be trees.
5 There .... be robots.
6 More people .... be astronauts.

2 ▶ **Talk to a friend. What do you think?**

> There won't be any cars.

> People will fly to work.

3 ▶ **Write P *(in the past)* or T *(today)* or F *(in the future)*.**

1 There are lots of cars. .....T.....
2 There won't be any water. ....
3 People didn't have computers. ....
4 There weren't any buses. ....
5 We might live on a different planet. ....
6 Every house has got a television. ....

4 ▶ Look and write.

work	be	buy	~~stay~~	live	fly

1 Will you ....*stay*.... at school until you are 18? ....
2 Will you .... in an office? ....
3 Will you .... to other countries? ....
4 Will you .... rich? ....
5 Will you .... a car? ....
6 Will you .... on the Moon? ....

5 ▶ Read the questions in exercise 4. Put a tick ✓, a cross ✗ or a question mark ? Then ask and answer.

✓ Yes, I will.
✗ No, I won't.
? I may / might.

Will you stay at school until you're 18?

Yes, I will.

6 ▶ Write sentences about you.

1 *I will stay at school until I'm 18.*
2 ....
3 ....
4 ....
5 ....
6 ....

We use may or might if we aren't sure about something.

I'll be a business-woman.

1 ▶ Match the words (1–6) with the examples (a–f).

1 ☐ determiner   2 ☐ pronoun   **a** job   **d** expensive

3 ☐ verb   4 ☐ preposition   **b** a lot   **e** fly

5 ☐ adjective   6 ☐ noun   **c** in   **f** her

2 ▶ Look and write the words from exercise 1.

1 She'll ......*fly*...... around the world. **(verb)**

2 She'll stay .... expensive hotels. **(preposition)**

3 She'll wear .... clothes. **(adjective)**

4 She'll speak .... of languages. **(determiner)**

5 Her .... will be very important. **(noun)**

6 Her secretary will go with .... **(pronoun)**

Remember! Think about which type of word could go in each gap.

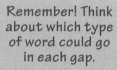

3 ▶ Circle the correct words.

When I leave school I'll **1 (go) / going** to university. I **2 will / won't** live at the university. I'll live with my friends in the town near the university. I'll stay there **3 when / until** I'm twenty-one, then I'll look for a **4 job / work.** I **5 can't / might** work in a hospital as a nurse or I might decide to be a teacher. I won't be rich, but I'll be happy **6 because / so** my job will be very interesting.

4 ▶ Look and write the words from exercise 1.

When I **1** .... school, I'll fly around the world and **2** .... in different countries. I'll work in schools and I'll teach English. I'll meet lots of interesting people. I'll make new friends and I'll learn to **3** .... their languages. I **4** .... be rich or famous, but I'll have an **5** .... time. I **6** .... write a book when I get home.

won't
excellent
live
speak
~~leave~~
might

Step 3 – Pass!

1 ▶ **Read the text. Choose the best words and write them on the lines.**

LIFE IN THE FUTURE

Example	What will the world be like in the future? ....*Will*............ life be the same?
1	Will we .... drive cars made of metal? Will we still read books
2	made of paper? Or will we all .... in houses on the Moon?
3	I believe that life will be very different in the future. We ....
	have televisions, radios or newspapers. We will watch films, listen to music
4	and read the...................................... on our computers. There won't be any
5	bookshops, because people won't buy books. .... read books
	on their computers, too.
6	People won't drive their cars .... computers will drive for
7	them. Cars might be slower and quieter .... they are today
8	and they won't be dangerous. People will go .... holiday in
	'space planes'. These will fly half way around the world in two hours.
	I think robots will work in factories and they will work for 24 hours a day. They
9	will be .... and faster than people. Medicines will be better
10	and people won't be ill very often. People might live .... they
	are 100 years old. I think life will be very different.

Example	(Will)	Does	Won't
1	just	still	already
2	live	living	will live
3	wouldn't	can't	won't
4	new	news	story
5	They'll	There	Their
6	until	when	because
7	than	then	that
8	in	at	on
9	cheapest	cheaper	more
10	always	when	until

1 ▶ **Write the words in the correct rooms.**

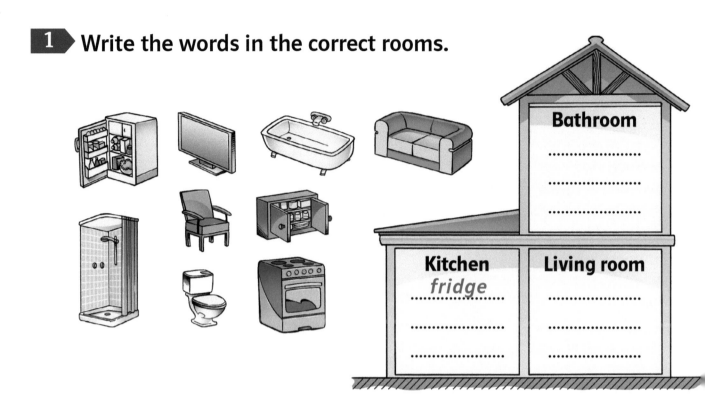

Bathroom
....
....
....

Kitchen
fridge
....
....

Living room
....
....
....

2 ▶ **Look and write the words.**

1 It's a room where there is a bath. ...*bathroom*...

2 It's something that you cook food on. ....

3 It's made of wood and you put books on it. ....

4 You sit on this when you watch TV. ....

5 You use this to make your hair tidy. ....

6 You turn this on when it's dark. ....

cooker
~~bathroom~~
light
shelf
sofa
comb

3 ▶ **Talk to a friend. Play a game.**

It's a place in the kitchen where you put food.

No! It's very cold.

Yes!

A cupboard?

A fridge?

4 ▶ Look and write the words.

> low ~~soft~~ empty dangerous faster dark

1 They didn't like the sofa because it was too hard. It wasn't
   ......_soft_...... enough.
2 There wasn't a window in the bathroom, so it was too ....
3 Be careful! The stairs are very old and ....
4 The television was on a .... shelf in the corner.
5 There wasn't any food in the fridge. It was ....
6 It's .... to have a shower than a bath, and it's better
   for the environment.

5 ▶ Look and read. Write *yes* or *no*.

1 The bedroom is very untidy. ...._yes_....
2 There are books on the shelf. ....
3 It's half past one. ....
4 The door is open. ....
5 The boy is wearing shorts. ....
6 There's a lamp on the desk. ....

6 ▶ Ask and answer.

What's your bedroom like?

It's big and it's usually untidy! There's a bed ...

43

1 **Circle the correct words.**

My friend Helen came to my house. She's always hungry so we got some flour, butter and chocolate. We **1** ate /(made) chocolate biscuits and cooked them in the **2** **oven / fridge.** My bedroom is on the first floor. Helen and I both love listening to **3** **the TV / music** so in the evening, we went **4** **upstairs / downstairs** to my bedroom and listened to some CDs. Helen stayed the night and at midnight we went downstairs. It was very quiet and **5** **light / dark.** Helen was afraid so we took a torch. We took the biscuits out of the fridge. Then we went back up to my **6** **bathroom / bedroom** and ate them all in bed!

To:

Subject:

Dear Anne

Thank you for having me to stay at your house last night. I had a great time. I **1** .... making chocolate biscuits and I liked **2** .... to music in your bedroom. I'm very tired **3** ....but it was great staying **4** .... until midnight and eating biscuits. They **5** .... very good in bed! Did I leave my new CD in your bedroom? Can you **6** .... it to school for me on Monday?

Have a good day!

Love Helen

Read the whole text before you decide which words are missing. You can use 1, 2, 3 or 4 words.

1 ▶ **Look at the picture and read the story. Write some words to complete the sentences about the story. You can use 1, 2, 3 or 4 words.**

The secret door

My name's Tom. Last week
I visited an old castle
with my class. We left early
in the morning and we went
by bus with our history
teacher. It took an hour
to get to the castle and
we sang songs on the bus.
It was very noisy!

We visited the castle
gardens. They were very interesting. Then we had lunch in the café. Then
we went inside the castle and visited all the old rooms. They were full
of old paintings. It was boring.

We were looking at the paintings when my friend Harry saw a secret door.
Harry and I waited until the room was empty and then we opened the door
and went inside. The door closed behind us and we couldn't open it. It
was very dark and we were afraid. We could see a small light far away.
'Follow the light,' I said, so Harry and I walked and walked.
At last we came to an open door and we walked outside. The bus was in
front of us. We ran to the bus. We were late so everyone was waiting for
us. 'Are you OK?' asked our teacher. 'We're fine, thanks,' we said. We
didn't tell anyone about our secret.

Example

Tom and his class went by bus to visit an .....*old castle*..... .

Questions

1 It was noisy on the bus because ....

2 Before lunch they ....

3 Harry saw the secret door when .... at the paintings.

4 Tom and Harry opened the door and went ....

5 They were afraid because ....

6 Everyone was waiting for them because ....

7 They told .... about their secret.

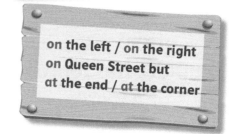

Step 1 – Prepare

1 ▶ Look and write the directions.

on the left / on the right
on Queen Street but
at the end / at the corner

 o_n_ t_h_e r_i_ _g_ h _t_

 s _ _ _ _ g_ t _ _ n

5 a_ th_ e_ _

 at _ h_ c_ _ n_ r

6 _ ur_ r i_ _ t

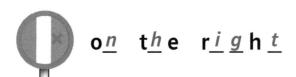 t_ _ n l_ _ t

7 _ n t_ _ l_ _ t

2 ▶ Look and read. Write the words.

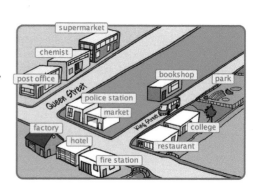

1 It's at the corner next to the college.
the restaurant

2 It's on Queen Street, on the left,
next to the supermarket.
....

3 The bus has just driven past it.
....

4 It's between the hotel and the bridge. ....

5 Look at the market. This place is on the left. ....

6 It's on the corner of Queen Street, next to the chemist. ....

3 ▶ Ask and answer.

It's next to the college.

The restaurant?

No.

The park?

Yes.

4 ▶ Look and circle *yes* or *no*.

1 The college is on Que[en] Street. **yes / no**

2 The bus is driving p[ast] the theatre. **yes / no**

3 The hotel is betwee[n] the factory and the restaurant. **yes / no**

4 The chemist is at the corner. **yes / no**

5 A car is driving over the bridge. **yes / no**

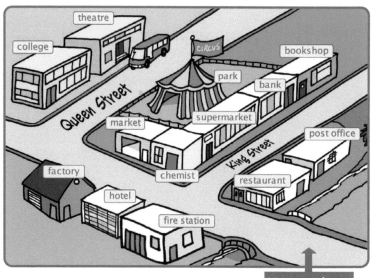

You are here

5 ▶ Look, read and write. **Where are you?**

1 Go over the bridge. Turn right and go straight on. It's at the end of the street on the left. *the bookshop*.

2 Go over the bridge. Go straight on. It's on the right next to the chemist. ....

3 Go over the bridge and go straight on. Go past the factory and turn right, it's on the corner on the left. ....

4 Go over the bridge. Go past the fire station. It's on the left next to the hotel. ....

5 Go over the bridge. Don't turn right. Go straight on. Go past the market and turn right. It's in the park on the right.

....

6 ▶ Talk to a friend. Play a game.

Excuse me. How do you get to the bookshop?

Go over the bridge, turn right and go straight on. It's at the end of the street on the left.

1 ▶ **Look at the picture and draw lines.**

1	He's flying	to the post office.
2	He's pointing	at the corner of the street.
3	The car is driving	between two shops.
4	The post office is	past the post office.
5	There's a lamp	next to the post office.
6	The purple shop is	above the street.

2 ▶ **Look, think and write.**

1 Who is going into the chemist? *A woman and her son*

2 What are they going to buy? ....

3 What is the boy carrying? ....

4 What has the man who is coming out of the bookshop bought? ....

5 Where is the girl on the bike going? ....

3 ▶ **Read and complete.**

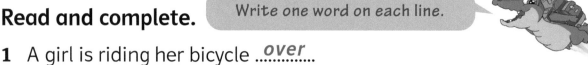

Write one word on each line.

1 A girl is riding her bicycle ....*over*.... the bridge.

2 The chemist is on the .... of the cinema.

3 A man is walking .... the police station.

4 A blue car is turning .... at the corner.

5 The post office is .... the police station.

1 ▶ **Read the letter and write the missing words.**
Write one word on each line.

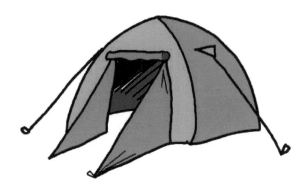

Dear Mum and Dad

Example   I ......*am*...... camping! The toilets are horrible and the showers are cold. Last night I lay down in my

1   .... and closed my eyes, but I

2   .... sleep. There were lots of insects in the

3   tent and it was noisy. I woke up very ....

because it was too light.

4   Tomorrow we're going to stay in a ....

5   It isn't cheap, it's .... We're going to have hot showers, we're going to eat in the restaurant and we're going to sleep in nice soft beds!

Love from

Richard

1 **Look and draw lines to match the opposite adjectives.**

1	empty	quiet
2	early	rich
3	married	closed
4	dark	boring
5	cheap	lovely
6	interesting	full
7	noisy	light
8	open	late
9	horrible	expensive
10	poor	single

2 **Look and write adjectives from exercise 1.**

1 On Sundays lots of shops aren't ...*closed*... .

2 I don't like history. It's .... It isn't ....

3 The bus wasn't .... It was .... of people.

4 On weekdays I get up .... for school. At the weekend
I stay in bed and I get up ....

5 In the summer the days are long. It's .... at 5.00 a.m.
and it's .... at 10.00 p.m.

6 At school we are very .... in the playground, but in the
library, we have to be ....

3 **Ask and answer.**

I think museums are interesting.

Do you? I think they're boring!

4 ▶ **Look and write. Then order the story A to D.**

every   rich   poor   secret   ~~gold~~   unhappy

☐ Then, one day the woman met the king at the secret place and he said 'I've got something for you.' He gave her a small box. Inside the box there was a **1** ....._gold_..... ring. The king and the woman were married. They lived together in the old castle on the hill.

☐ The king wrote a letter and put it in an envelope with a map. He sent the letter to the young woman's address. The woman opened the envelope and read the letter. It said 'Look at the map. Meet me at the **2** .... place.'

☐ The young woman went to the secret place and the king was waiting for her. They walked and they talked and soon they were good friends. They met **3** .... day for a month.

|A| Many years ago, a king lived in an old castle on a hill. He had lots of money and he was very **4** .... , but he was **5** .... One day he was riding his horse in the woods when he saw a beautiful woman. She was very **6** .... and she lived in small house. He followed her back to her little house and wrote down the address.

5 ▶ **Look and write *so* or *because*.**

1 The man was rich ....._because_..... he was the king.

2 The young woman was poor .... she didn't live in a big house.

3 The king followed her .... he wanted her address.

4 He needed her address .... he wanted to send her a letter.

6 ▶ **Look and write Who, Where, Why, How, What. Then ask and answer.**

1 ....._Who_..... was rich but unhappy?

2 .... was the king doing when he saw the young woman?

3 .... did the poor woman live?

4 .... did the king follow her?

Who was rich but unhappy?

The king.

7 ▶ Reading & Writing

Step 2 – Practise

1 ▶ Read and draw lines to make part of a story.

1   Robert followed Harry   and saw Grandfather.
2   Harry was carrying   up the stairs.
3   Suddenly they heard   sleeping in a chair!
4   It sounded like   a torch.
5   They opened the door   a lion.
6   He was   a strange noise.

2 ▶ Read and tick ✓ the best words to complete the sentences.

1   Harry had a torch
    ☑ because it was dark.
    ☐ so it was dark.

2   They walked slowly
    ☐ outside.
    ☐ upstairs.

3   They were afraid because
    ☐ he opened the door.
    ☐ they heard a strange noise.

4   It sounded
    ☐ like an animal.
    ☐ like Grandfather.

5   When they got to the top of the stairs they
    ☐ opened the door.
    ☐ closed the door.

6   Grandfather
    ☐ were in bed.
    ☐ was sleeping.

3 ▶ Look and write the words.

| pushed | ~~dark~~ | sleeping | laughed | following | sounded |

It was ❶ ....*dark*........ . Robert had a torch. I was
❷ .... Robert up the stairs when we heard
a noise. It ❸ .... like a lion. We were afraid.
We came to a door. Robert ❹ .... the door
open slowly. Then he ❺ .... It wasn't a lion.
It was his grandfather. He was ❻ .... in a chair.

1 ▶ Look at the three pictures. Write about this story.
Write 20 or more words.

....

....

....

....

....

....

....

....

....

....

Step 1 – Prepare

1 ▶ Find these things in the pictures. Draw a line to match.

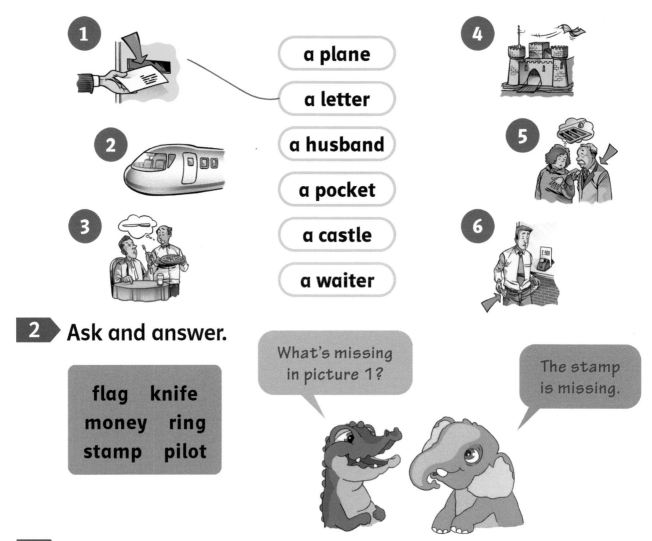

a plane

a letter

a husband

a pocket

a castle

a waiter

2 ▶ Ask and answer.

flag   knife
money   ring
stamp   pilot

What's missing in picture 1?

The stamp is missing.

3 ▶ Look at exercise 1. Read, circle and write.

1 Is the man posting a postcard? No, he's posting ......*a letter*...... .
   an email   (a letter)   a present
2 Where is the pilot? Is he early? No, he's ....
   excited   bored   late
3 Is the waiter carrying a cake? No, he's carrying a ....
   biscuit   pizza   sweets
4 Are there spots on the flag? No, there are ....
   letters   pictures   stripes
5 Are they married? Yes, they are. She's his ....
   wife   surname   husband
6 Is the watch cheap? No, it's ....
   dangerous   expensive   soft

4 ▶ Listen and number the pictures in order. 🔊 22

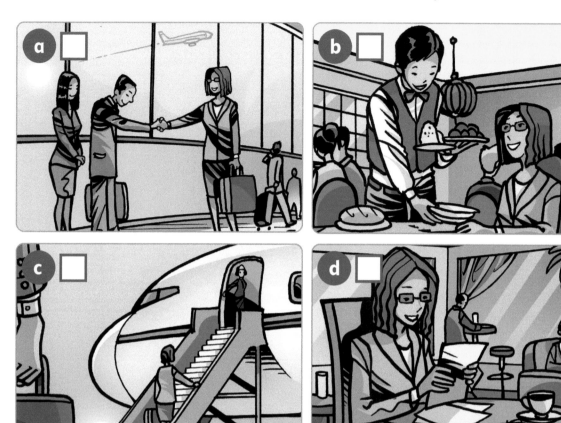

5 ▶ Write the words in order to make questions.

1 Mrs Brown / Why / go / airport / to / the / did / ?
Why did Mrs Brown go to the airport?

2 did / she / her / with / take / What / ?
....

3 travel / How / she / did / ?
....

4 airport / did / she / Who / at / meet / the / ?
....

5 have / dinner / she / Where / did / ?
....

6 read / When / she / the / letter / did / ?
....

6 ▶ Ask and answer.

Why did Mrs Brown go to the airport?

Because she had to go to a meeting.

Step 2 – Practise

1 ▸ **Look at picture A. Find these and circle.**

1 It's an old castle.
2 They're married.
3 She's wearing a gold ring.
4 The taxi door is closed.
5 There's a flag.
6 There are two suitcases.

2 ▸ **Look at picture B. Put a tick ✓ or a cross ✗.**

Draw a clear tick or cross inside the box!

1 ☐ The man standing next to the taxi isn't the woman's husband.

2 ☐ The flag has got a stripe with a spot on it.

3 ☐ The hotel door is open.

4 ☐ The taxi driver is carrying two suitcases.

5 ☐ The man's wife is sitting in the taxi.

6 ☐ There's a castle on the hill.

4 **Look at the pictures and make questions. Then match them to the answers.**

1 Which country / Mr Peters / visit last week?
Which country did Mr Peters visit last week?
....

2 How / he / travel? ....

3 What colour / his suitcase? ....

4 What / happen / in his hotel room? ....

5 How / he / find / Mrs Wilkins' address? ....

6 Where / he and Mrs Wilkins / meet? ....

a In the hotel restaurant. ....

b It was blue. ....

c There was a letter in the suitcase. ....

d America. ....*1*....

e By plane. ....

f He saw that he had the wrong suitcase! ....

5 **Match the pictures in exercise 3 and the sentences.**

1 Oh, no! This isn't my suitcase. Here's an envelope. I'll find the phone number for this address. ....*c*....

2 When I get to the hotel, I'm going to have a swim! ....

3 Hello, Mr Peters. Thank you for bringing my suitcase! ....

4 I'm going to America! Here's my suitcase. ....

Step 3 – Pass!

1 ▶ **Find the differences.**

Information

	A Jane	B Robert
Where / going to go next summer?	camping	?
How / going to go there?	by train	?
What / going to take?	a rucksack with a tent	?
Who / going to go with?	her class	?
Who / going to go with?	go swimming, visit a castle	?

Story

Part 1 (5 questions)

Listen and draw lines. There is one example. 🔊 23

Sarah   David   Michael   Helen

Harry   Emma   Katy   William

Listening

Part 2 (5 questions)

Listen and write. There is one example. 🔊 24

AN INTERESTING JOB

Name: .... *Martyn* ....

1 How old: ....

2 Job: ....

3 Name of club: ....

4 Date of next game: ....

5 Time: ....

Part 3 (5 questions)

What did each person buy at the market?
Listen and write a letter in each box. There is one example. 🔊 25

Mrs Swan [C]

Mr Swan [ ]

Harry [ ]

Katy [ ]

Richard [ ]

Sarah [ ]

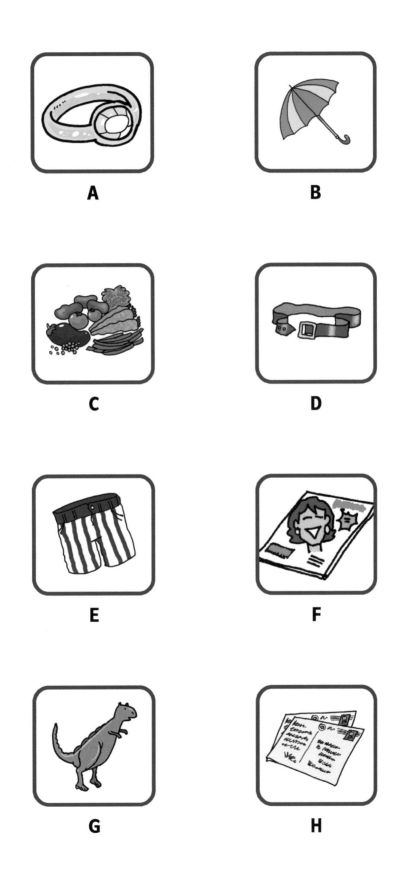

A

B

C

D

E

F

G

H

Part 4 (5 questions)

Listen and tick ✓ the box. There is one example. 🔊 26

What's the weather like?

A   B ☐   C ☐

1 Which snowman has Betty made?

A ☐   B ☐   C ☐

2 Where is she going to go?

3 Who is she going to meet?

A ☐ B ☐ C ☐

4 What is she going to take?

A ☐ B ☐ C ☐

5 What time does she have to come home?

  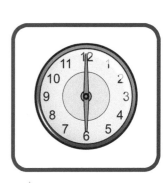

A ☐ B ☐ C ☐

Part 5 (5 questions)

Listen and colour and write. There is one example. 🔊 27

Practice Test

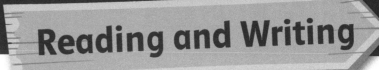
Part 1 (10 questions)

Look and read. Choose the correct words and write them on the lines. There is one example.

butterfly

fog

wood

queen

rocket

ring

scissors

sledge

glue

swan

camel

torch

waiter

wool

king

Example

You wear this with your trousers
or jeans if they are too big.   *belt*

Questions

1 It's a beautiful, big, white bird with
   a long neck. It swims on a lake. ....

2 It takes astronauts up into space. ....

3 He brings your meals
   in a restaurant.   ....

4 It will help you see in the dark. ....

5 You can ride on it down a
   mountain in the snow.   ....

6 In this weather, you can't
   see very well.   ....

7 Sweaters, scarves, hats and
   gloves are made of it.   ....

8 She lives in a castle.   ....

9 You use these to cut paper,
   card or plastic.   ....

10 It's a pretty insect.
    It's got four wings.   ....

Part 2 (5 questions)

Harry is talking to his friend, Betty. What does Harry say?
Read the conversation and choose the best answer.
Write a letter (A–H) for each answer. You do not need to use all the letters.

Example

Harry: Hi, Betty! What are you going to do today?

Betty: .... C ....

Questions

1 **Harry:** Why?

Betty: ....

2 **Harry:** Are you going to draw a picture on it?

Betty: ....

3 **Harry:** What kind of picture?

Betty: ....

4 **Harry:** Here's a nice one. Look, it's a rabbit.

Betty: ....

5 **Harry:** Of course. Have you got a pair of scissors?

Betty: ....

A Yes, I like it. Can you cut it out for me?

B She likes animals. Perhaps I'll find something in this animal magazine.

C I'm going to make a card for Sarah.

D No, I'm going to cut out a picture from a magazine.

E Yes, I have. Here you are.

F Because it's her birthday tomorrow.

G No, I don't.

H No, it isn't.

Part 3 (5 questions)

Read the story. Choose a word from the box. Write the correct word next to the numbers 1–5. There is one example.

Example

> hotel   cooker   lovely   dream   expensive
> fire   photo   rained   raining   stars

Last summer, we went on holiday in the countryside. We didn't want to stay in a ....*hotel*....... because it was too **1** .... We wanted to sleep outside, under the **2** .... , in a tent! So we drove to the mountains and found a quiet place next to the river. We cooked our dinner on a **3** .... that night. We told stories and sang songs. It was fun! When we got tired, my dad said, 'Time to go to bed! Let't get up early in the morning and go for a swim in the river!' That night, I had a **4** .... I was swimming in the river. The water felt cold ... Suddenly I woke up. It wasn't a dream! There was water inside our tent! It was **5** .... very hard, and the tent was wet. My dad went outside the tent – and walked into the water! The river was very deep – there was water all around our tent. We packed our tents up and drove to a hotel. That was the end of our camping holiday!

6 **Now choose the best name for the story. Tick ✓ one box.**

A holiday by the sea ☐

A terrible fire ☐

My camping trip ☐

Part 4 (10 questions)

Read the text. Choose the right words and write them on the lines.

Butterflies

Example   There ....*are*........ many different kinds of butterflies in

1   the world. Butterflies are .... of different colours. One

2   butterfly is called the Zebra butterfly .... it's got wings

3   black and white striped wings! In spring, you .... see lots

4   of butterflies .... the garden. They drink from flowers.

5   They also .... fruit.

6   Butterflies like warm places. Lots of butterflies leave ....
    home countries in the winter and they fly to a warmer country.

7   They don't live .... a long time – eleven months is very
    old for a butterfly.

8   Butterflies can see lots of different colours, ... their

9   favourite colours are red, white and pink. They can see ....

10   colours very well. They .... taste with their mouths.
     They taste with their feet!

Example	is	(are)	be
1	some	one	lots
2	but	because	how
3	can	do	are
4	on	at	in
5	play	go	like
6	them	they	their
7	in	for	to
8	so	but	because
9	these	this	that
10	not	don't	don't like

Part 5 (7 questions)

**Look at the picture and read the story.
Write some words to complete the sentences
about the story. You can use 1, 2, 3 or 4 words.**

Shell soup

One day a man went to a village. He was carrying a large, empty, metal bowl.

He didn't have any food, so he was very hungry. But the people in the village were poor. They didn't have much food, and they were usually very weak and hungry, too. They said, "We are sorry, but we don't have any food to give you."

So the man went to the beach and filled the bowl with sea water. He picked up a shell from the beach and put it into the bowl. He put the bowl on a fire to cook.

A farmer from the village looked at the man. "What are you cooking?" he asked. The man said, "It's shell soup."

The farmer asked, "Can we have some?"

The man said, "Yes, you can. But shell soup tastes better with some vegetables. Have you got just one vegetable to put into the soup?"

So the farmer gave the man a carrot and he put it into the bowl to cook with the shell. Then the farmer's wife put a potato into the bowl.

Soon, all the people in the village started to smell the soup and came to see what the man was cooking. They all brought one vegetable to put into the soup: a tomato, an onion, a few beans and some peas.

When the soup was ready, the man said, "Everybody, bring a spoon to eat the soup. Come and have some lovely soup."

Everybody enjoyed the soup and said thank you to the man. After that, they were never hungry again. They ate shell soup often and they were healthy and strong.

Examples

A man went .....*to a village*..... one day.

He was carrying a bowl .....*made of metal*..... .

Questions

1 The man was hungry because he .... any food.

2 He got some .... the sea and put it into the bowl.

3 On the sand, he found .... and put it into the bowl, too.

4 He started cooking on ....

5 The people in the village could .... something nice cooking.

6 They all put a .... the bowl.

7 Then they all brought .... the soup, and it was very nice.

Part 6 (5 questions)

Read the letter and write the missing words.
Write one word on each line.

Dear Grandma

Example I'm ......*going*...... to visit a museum with my class next week!

1 Our .... , Miss Smith, wants to show us all the

2 interesting things there. I'm very .... about the trip, because I like learning about history.

We're going to travel to the museum by bus. We aren't going to eat in the museum restaurant, so we

3 have to take our .... in our rucksacks.

4 Mum is going to make me my .... food: a chicken sandwich!

5 I'll .... a postcard at the museum and put a stamp on it. Then I'll write and tell you all about the day.

Love Sarah

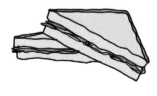

Part 7

Look at the three pictures. Write about this story.
Write 20 or more words.

....
....
....
....
....
....
....
....
....
....

Summary of Procedures

The usher introduces the child to the examiner. The examiner asks the child's name and how old the child is.

Information for the "examiner"

1

The examiner shows the child the candidate's copy of the Find the Differences picture. The child is initially shown the examiner's copy as well, then encouraged to look at the candidate's copy only. The examiner then makes a series of statements about the examiner's picture and the child has to respond by making statements showing how the candidate's picture is different, for example In my picture, a boy is reading a book about London, and the child answers In my picture, a boy is reading a book about Paris.

2

The examiner shows the child the candidate's copy of the Information Exchange. The child is initially shown the examiner's copy as well, then encouraged to look at the candidate's copy only. The examiner then asks the child questions related to the information the child has, for example Where is Emma going shopping? and the child answers. The child then asks the examiner questions, for example What does David want to buy? and the examiner answers.

3

The examiner tells the child the name of the story and describes the first picture, for example Making a cake. Katy and Emma are going to make a cake. Katy has got some eggs, flour and butter. The examiner then asks the child to continue telling the story.

4

The examiner asks questions about the child, for example What time do you get up in the morning?

Speaking

Find the difference

Information gap

A David's shopping trip

A David		B Emma	
Where / go shopping?	at the supermarket	Where / go shopping?	?
What / he / want to buy?	some soap	What / she / want to buy?	?
Why?	for his mum's birthday	Why?	?
What / smell like?	flowers	What / feel like?	?
he / buy it? Why?	yes, because his mum loves things that smell nice	she / buy it? Why not?	?

B Emma's shopping trip

A David		B Emma	
Where / go shopping?	?	Where / go shopping?	in the market
What / he / want to buy?	?	What / she / want to buy?	a hat
Why?	?	Why?	because the weather was getting colder
What / smell like?	?	What / feel like?	soft and warm
he / buy it? Why?	?	she / buy it? Why not?	no, because it was getting too expensive

Picture story

Making a cake

Practise and Pass
Young Learners English Test
FLYERS

....

took the Practise and Pass Flyers Test on

....

at

....

Listening ☆ ☆ ☆ ☆ ☆

Reading & Writing ☆ ☆ ☆ ☆ ☆

Speaking ☆ ☆ ☆ ☆ ☆

Signed

....

Test checklist

Are you ready for the test?

✗ / ? / ✓

Before the test

Learn your words. .... ☐

Practise your spelling. .... ☐

Say words in English. .... ☐

Get a pencil, rubber and crayons! .... ☐

During the test

Look at the clock. .... ☐

Answer all the questions. .... ☐

Write neatly. .... ☐

At the end of the test

Check your answers. .... ☐

Can you see a mistake? Use your
rubber and write it correctly. .... ☐

Don't worry! You're a good student!

Learn your words

Which animals can you see? Number the pictures and circle the animal that is extinct.

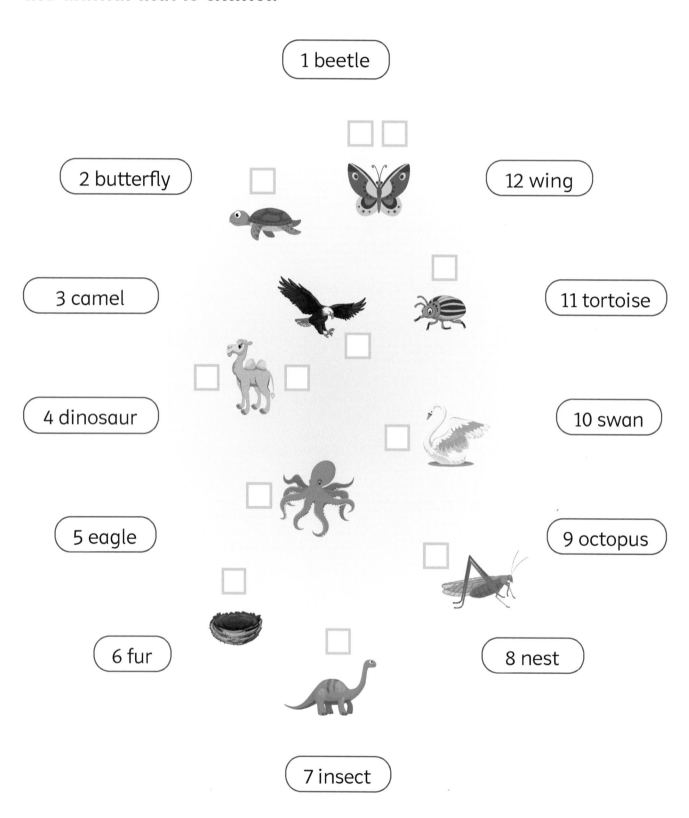

1 beetle

2 butterfly

12 wing

3 camel

11 tortoise

4 dinosaur

10 swan

5 eagle

9 octopus

6 fur

8 nest

7 insect

Learn your words

Find the word and write the number. Circle four things you use to eat with.

1 biscuit	2 butter	3 cereal	4 chopsticks	5 flour	6 fork
7 honey	8 jam	9 knife	10 olives	11 pepper	12 pizza
13 salt	14 spoon	15 strawberry	16 sugar	17 yoghurt

Learn your words

Label the pictures and write the numbers in the correct column.

inside	inside and outside	outside

1 brush   2 comb   3 cooker   4 cushion   5 fridge

6 gate   7 oven   8 screen   9 shampoo   10 shelf

11 soap   12 steps   13 swing   14 telephone   15 bandage

What's it made of?

Write the words in the sentences.

 1  2  3  4   5

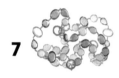 6   7  8 9

1 It's made of .... It's a ....

2 It's made of .... It's a ....

3 It's made of .... It's a ....

4 It's made of .... It's a ....

5 It's made of ....

6 They're made of .... They're ....

7 It's made of .... It's a ....

8 It's made of paper. It's a ....

9 They're made of .... They're ....

bracelet   card   crown   glass
glove   gold   key   metal   necklace
plastic   pyjamas   silver   spotted
striped   sunglasses

Learn your words

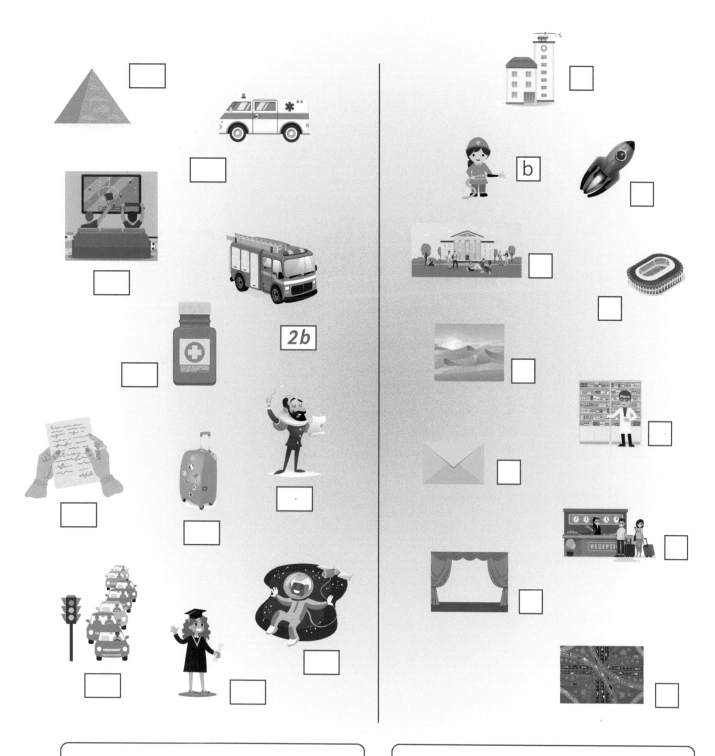

1 ambulance **2** fire engine
3 pyramid **4** letter
5 medicine **6** football match
7 actor **8** astronaut
9 traffic **10** suitcase **11** student

a hospital **b** fire fighter
c spaceship **d** university
e stadium **f** desert
g chemist shop
h envelope **i** hotel **j** stage
k motorway

Learn your words

Opposites

Make word pairs.

14   12   ☐ ☐   ☐ ☐

☐ ☐   ☐ ☐   ☐ ☐

☐ ☐   ☐ ☐   ☐ ☐

1 interested   2 left   3 alone   4 bored
5 cheap   6 heavy   7 dark   8 empty   9 expensive
10 full   11 hard   12 high   13 light   14 low
15 right   16 light   17 soft   18 together

89

Learn your words

Which places can you see? Number the pictures.

  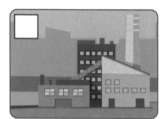

- 1 airport
- 2 stadium
- 3 castle
- 4 police station
- 5 restaurant
- 6 bank
- 7 theatre
- 8 fire station
- 9 hotel
- 10 post office
- 11 factory
- 12 skyscraper
- 13 museum
- 14 bridge

Learn your words

In the classroom

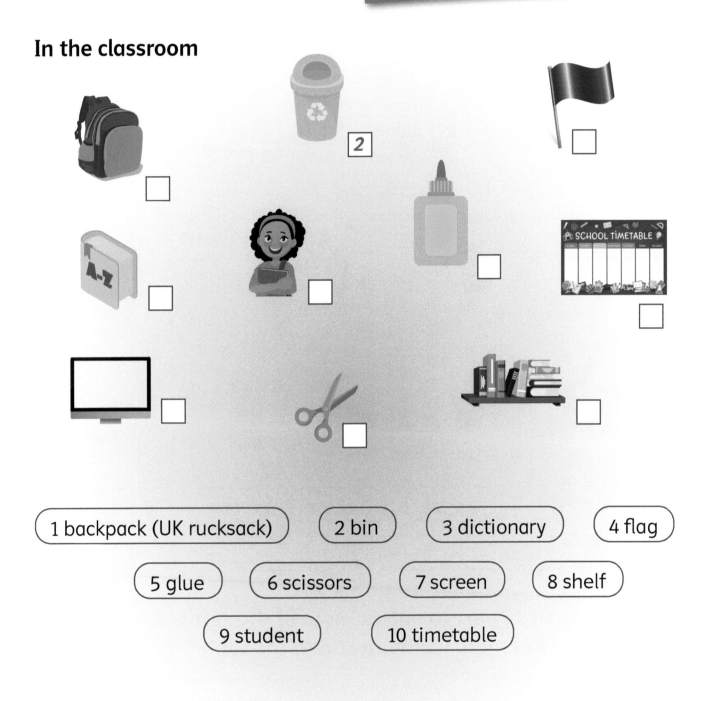

1 backpack (UK rucksack)　　2 bin　　3 dictionary　　4 flag

5 glue　　6 scissors　　7 screen　　8 shelf

9 student　　10 timetable

School subjects

Tick your favourite subject. Put a cross by a subject you don't like.

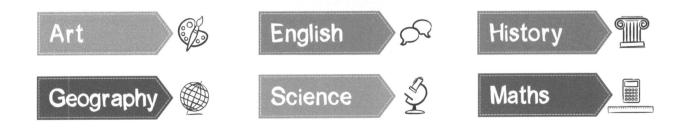

Art

English

History

Geography

Science

Maths

91

Learn your words

Match a picture with a word.

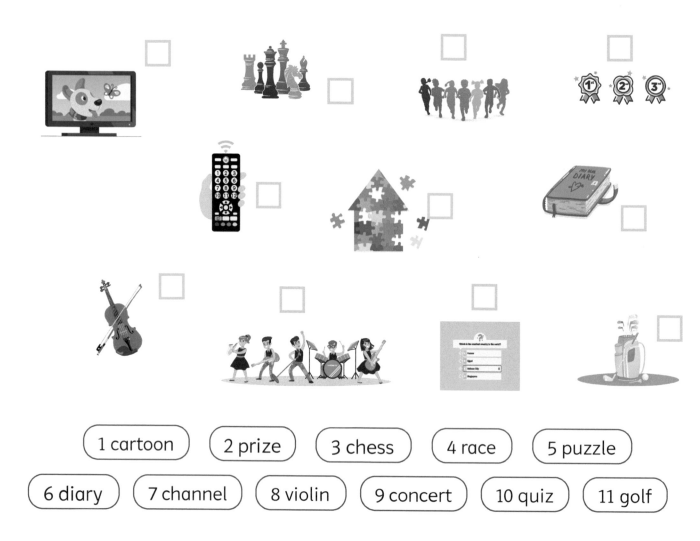

(1 cartoon) (2 prize) (3 chess) (4 race) (5 puzzle)

(6 diary) (7 channel) (8 violin) (9 concert) (10 quiz) (11 golf)

Write the activity next to one or more of the verbs in the table. Can you think of more words to add to the table?

listen to	
watch	
write	
read	
play	
do	
change	
run	
win	

Learn your words

Match jobs (1–9) and things or places (a–i).

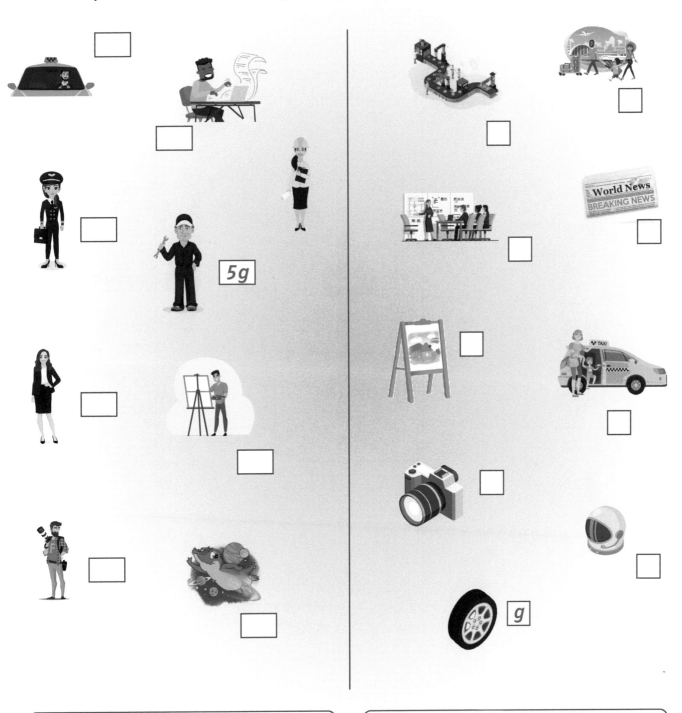

5g

g

---

1 astronaut   **2** pilot
3 journalist   **4** businesswoman
5 mechanic   **6** taxi driver
7 artist   **8** engineer
9 photographer

a passenger   **b** painting
c camera   **d** newspaper
e helmet   **f** meeting
g wheel   **h** factory   **i** airport

Which words can your see? Number the pictures.

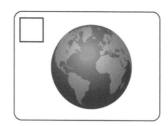
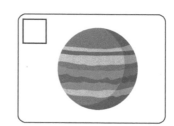

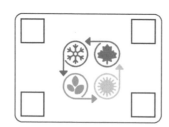
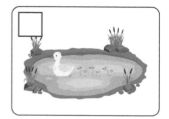
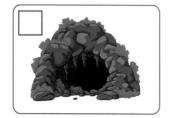
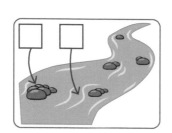

1 air   2 water   3 cave   4 Earth   5 fire

6 hill   7 spring   8 ocean   9 planet

10 pond   11 autumn   12 space   13 stone

14 stream   15 summer   16 winter   17 environment

Learn your words

What's he like?

Go away!

See you next week!

What else do we need?

What time does the film start?

Excellent!

... if you want.

You're welcome!

In a minute!

That's amazing!

No problem!

Images